Wet Spots
&
Tear Drops

Justine Monikue

ISBN 978-0615544441

Written and Edited by Justine Monikue
Cover Design by Justine Monikue

Visit jfilez.wordpress.com

Dedicated to my mutti, Marsha.
Thanks for believing in my craft, and loving me.

Contents

Mine Orts

Hearts

Wednesday Night's Dinner Special
Your Stupidity is Embarrassing Both of Us
She Eats from His Plate and Samples Others

Bed Sheets

Doxy of the Opaque
False Advertisement
Hot Silhouette
My Favorite Position
The Prettiest Hooker I Know
Virgin Cocktail

Tears

Sparkless
Seasons of Amity
Intersextion
Descension to Hades
Black Bombazine
Heavy Things

Cue Cards

What Shall I Do With My Eyes?
The Bright Side
Yes, You're a Pagan
About Spiders
The Report Card
Labels

Spots

Mine Orts

30B

After years of wearing
34B
34A
and
32A
bras,
I have finally uncovered,
through proper measurement,
what my actual bust size is!
What a relief.
Now I understand
why I always get carded.
Now I know
why I can't find my size,
in the Women's Intimates section;
because it's in the Girls' department,
on the racks with the training bras.

Cheers to kiwis!

No, I'm Not Twenty-Seven

No, I'm not twenty-seven.

I was not born in the 80s.

I do not remember when Care Bears were fluffy,
Strawberry Shortcake was plump, and Eddie
Murphy was funny.

I never had a Nintendo, Sega, or played Pac-
Man for hours.

No, I didn't stay up after my bedtime to watch
Def Comedy Jam or Arsenio Hall.

Who's this Milli Vanilli you speak of? Sounds
like a retired ice cream flavor from Baskin-
Robbins.

LaToya Jackson? In Playboy? Ya Don't Say.
No, I don't recall when that happened.

Who told you "The Power" by Snap! is one of my
favorite songs?

You also heard "Tom Sawyer" by Rush is a track
I fancy too? You're being slightly
slanderous, aren't you?

How would I possibly know all the names of the
members of New Kids on the Block or Boyz II
Men?

No, I don't think synthesizers and Bermuda bags are awesome.

I've never seen a high-top fade in all my life.

Acid wash jeans sound quite dangerous.

It isn't nice to tease hair.

I keep telling you that I'm not twenty-seven.

I'm actually twenty-seven years, two days, three hours, and six minutes old.

And for the record, high top sneakers NEVER went out of style.

My Hair Is Me

Having an afro is unusual apparently.
People assume I'm not from America,
but from parts of Africa.

I love my hair,
every curly kink.

I love knowing
I'm in a country
where I can
be myself without
breaking a law,
where I can
dress like a
fashionista or swap meet rat.

I love how I can wear
my hair any way I please.
However, it shouldn't be
assumed that my hair
is making a political statement,
or posing for a flag of another nation.

My follicles.
My natural crown.
My pride.
Me.

Truce

I won't call you a spendthrift,
if you don't call me cheap.
You are still an ogre,
and for that,
I don't apologize.

Winter Plague

I used to be a four-seasoned kind of girl,
but now I'm a one-season woman.
The thermostat is low,
and so is my patience.
My snow boots run high,
along with frozen tension.
A gun is useless,
since you can't shoot cold.

Winter is an icey son of a bitch that lives in
his father's basement.
He is so unforgiving and at times power
hungry,
eating away at the lives of others.
Reducing thriving organisms to merciful
servants.
I wouldn't give a shit about having thermals
and an endless supply of cocoa,
but old Jack says,
this is the hand I've been dealt,
so play 'em with a straight face!
I'll play alright.
With my bottle of rum.
A pack of tube socks.
A wool beret.
And a pink zebra Snuggie knock-off.

I want nothing more to do with the old man,
Unless he's willing to front the bill for the
oil.

Down Trodden

You see me,
head down,
face to pebbles,
casting stones at my conscience.
I know I'm better,
than what they think.
I know I'm wiser,
than what they've heard,
though I always wonder,
if the world's a lie,
and I'm the truth.

I am not going to settle for fakery.
I am not going to ignore the obvious.
I refuse to be taken for granted, and shown
anything less than respect.
I am a queen in my own right, and so I should
be treated as such.
Bowing down without good cause is no reason to
contrive going under.
If I am not accepted for who and what I am
wholeheartedly, by those who seek me, then I
must vanish from their space, and seek solace
in my own, for what's worse than wasting time,
is wasting thought on those who waste heart.

5.12

The day I lost my sanity
The day I gained new perspective
The day I discovered comfort
The day I obtained worry
The day I lost faith
The day I renewed hope
The day I lost my appetite
The day I craved endlessly
The day I lost my way
The day I sought another path
The day I was adrift
The day I found cover
The day my heart broke
The day it mended

The day I lost a brother.

The day I gained a son.

The day of annual wretch and jubilation.

Twice Bitten Zombie

The first time,
I remember,
was at a round glass table.
I had failed you,
again.
Your rage permeated the conjoined rooms,
my shame dissipated beneath the floorboards.
You would have aborted me,
if you knew I'd be more trouble
than I was worth.

The second instance,
I recall,
was on a floor of black tiles.
I was playing defense,
again.
Your fury engulfed the kitchen,
my resentment hovered above the ceiling fan.
You wished I had been buried,
after bouts of illness,
rather than *the one* who was.

To hope for my breath to cease,
to pray for my blood to thin,
to dream of my demise,
are symptoms of a barren soul,
lost in the universe of time and self-pity.

Unlikely it is to give life,
while banishing it from thriving,
in your mass of opaque visions,
and threadbare chasms of hypocrisy.

If I'm a Rebel, Than Satan's a Savior

I'm not a rebel,
because I clip your ridged nails
and scrub your singed flesh.
I can't be a rebel,
since I wear dresses,
with hemlines of unbleached cotton,
and shoes of wasted burlap cloth.
Rebels do not piss in
toilets of Moët,
and wash their hands
in gold rimmed basins.
Rebels won't cry out,
even when an aged machete
has shuffled each part
of their body.
BUT,
Maybe I am a rebel,
for the only
blood I see,
is on
Mary.

One Curly Gray Hair

You've been sprouting in the same spot for
years now.
I'm not even thirty yet, but this does not
matter to you.
It's your mission to let me know you're there,
camping on my scalp, in protest of youth.
I don't mind you though, though I don't know
you.

I admit when we first met, I was intimidated,
mostly from my own assumptions that you were
setting up my head for a party, where many
other curly gray hairs would attend.

I'm a one-on-one kind of chick, and prefer to
keep to myself as much as possible.
I see we both have this in common.

I'm glad you don't get sore when I need a
trim; you seem to understand the importance of
good grooming habits, and I respect you for
that.

Besides, you are a minority amongst my other
follicles, the curly black hairs, and this
makes you a star.

Yes, a star.

People notice you and sometimes tug your
shoulder, or pat you like a good boy.
You don't like it, but you like the attention.

So mademoiselle, you need not question if I'll
paint you, in an attempt to assimilate you.
No.
Never.
Just don't invite any other gray curls to the
neighborhood.

Yard Sale of Broken Dreams

On the small, lightly scratched, second hand
oak coffee table, every centimeter is filled
with failed relationships, dashed hopes for
the future, and bad decisions.

Having a gunshot wedding a month and a half
before the arrival of my first child-$4

The two month love triangle-$10

Getting arrested for assault and battery-$7

Being unemployed with an MFA at age twenty-
seven-$3

To the left, on an orange milk crate, is a
mason jar full of grudges going for ten cents
a piece, though the one I had against my
maternal half, sits in a ten ounce Coke
bottle, for eight thousand dollars.

The Tiger Calling the Panther Catty

You call me crazy, before I remind you that insanity runs on your side of the family.

You call me lazy, after I've witnessed you slithering about daily, in your uniform of slippers and a housecoat.

You call me deaf, though you seem to read lips and I cannot.

You call me dumb, and then ask me how to spell common words.

You keep phoning me, but I'm screening your calls.

Two Zero Zero Four

Little sparrow, sing
in the dim morning light
of my brother,
seventeen years old, gone
born abroad
in the land of Jager
and boiling pots
of kielbasa, filling the
nostrils with angst and hunger,
though you didn't know
and didn't care.

Little sparrow, sing
in the dim morning light
of my brother,
the gifted jester
and great debater,
who cursed while
succumbing to the
magic of Marinol
in the bed of death
with no pillows.

Little sparrow, sing
in the dim morning light
of my brother,
the king of pain
and the prince
of harmed flesh,
back to your birthplace
which is also
your gate of departure,
may the ale be sweeter than you,

my transparent angel.

Hearts

Lovely

What does it mean to love?
To coat words with saccharine,
to sweep the dust of clouds,
surpassing the waning moon,
or to lull the tiresome sun,
who breathes in
the air of Earth,
filled with hydrogen nectar,
and diamond sighs.

Ash

I weep in the wind of the rooster's call,
lying ever so still in my Egyptian cotton
sheets,
now soaked with tears of lust and anguish,
because I want you,
and may never have you.
You rule the darker side of the moon,
with angel food cake cheeks,
peppercorn pupils,
mango lips,
and star anise skin.
It would be unjust to demand
a change in you,
to emphasize the light side of the sun,
since you fear the impending ash
that falls off the surface,
carrying you with it,
and my unrequited fancy.

Clash Then Crash

We began, like a budding poppy,
so new, and filled with pollenated nuance.
Though as we grew,
we grew apart.
But that's just how it is when you're young,
you're still floating among the skies,
bouncing off every cloud,
trying to figure out which one is right for
you:
cumulus
cirrus
or stratus?
Then it comes down to seasons:
falling leaf
wintery wind
summery sand
or springy dew?
You are a moon man,
and she, a sun woman,
and the two shall never meet,
sans the tonic eclipse,
where they clash,
then crash.

Enchanting Myopia

Skin of honey suckle, teeth of narcissus,
lashes of rye, and bones of Teflon make
him,
her,
this person, an invaluable oddity.

I'll take you, all of you,
with no regard to gender,
no regard to identity,
no regard to anything,
but the paroxysm betwixt us.

Every Hetero Man's Fantasy

It's hard enough to remember keeping your legs
crossed,
Or to keep those furry beasts above your eyes
arched,
But to insist on being this debutante dream,
Is more than I can digest,
For my absent mind and translucent heart,
Don't give a damn about what a man
Wants
Thinks
Likes
Sees
Expects
or needs
In a *real* woman that walks the Earth, with
Patent pumps
Tanned roots
Glossy molars
Pop curves
Suede toes
And a doll face.
I guess that's what happens when you're a
lifelong subscriber to Swank
And a regular at The Gold Club in Wilmington.
You forge your dull realities into
drizzling dreams of pole dancing
and homemaking,
Which is only a glitzy goal
That will never
materialize
before you,
Unless your name is Hugh Hefner.

I'm Smokn' All Your Cigarettes

I'm smokn' all your cigarettes,
and drinkn' all your booze.
Cuz I just found out,
she's layn' next to you.
I'm shreddn' all your shirts,
and selln' all your shoes.
Cuz I just found out,
you were never true.

So you wanna two-time me baby?
So you wanna see me go crazy?
Well I'm a woman of my word,
haven't you heard?
Well I'm a woman of my day,
you hear what I say?
I don't leave promises left undone,
I don't have to be out on the run,
just to tell everyone,
that in this dirty house,
you're the filthy one!

So I'm smokn' all your cigarettes.
Drinkn' all your booze.
Burnin' all your jeans,
and eatn' all your food.

Laughter Doesn't Hurt

When you left me,
I chuckled.

When you cut my face out your pictures,
I snickered.

When you had me arrested,
I howled.

When you had me fired,
I chortled.

When you stabbed me,
I roared.
I roared so shrilly,
allowing the blood,
mingled with bottled tears,
to spray all over the cheap linoleum floor.

The Wait

I slump over my shadow,
wondering if you got the message,
or chose to ignore it.
I can't ignore the
beating of my lab rat heart,
when I get a tiny peek at you,
or the trillion thoughts, of
chai tea kisses
and red licorice hugs,
that I want to share
with you, until
all the clocks
of the world
perish, in an
upheaval, of
wasted time.

Train of Thought

She waved goodbye to her old lover,
a lover filled with endless triumphs and
intentions,
towards the girl shrinking at the window.
He recalled, with a slight smile,
the magnificence of her pectin lips,
marshmallow breasts, and fondant backside.

So many morning romps, afternoon delights, and
late night snacks,
kept him full throughout their time together.

As the young woman lowered her waving hand,
she drifted back to the last sheet session,
where her tears hydrated her pending loss,
of a man that did not truly belong to her.

He flagged her one last time with a stifled
hand,
as the train moved on towards his old life,
the life he had evaded,
in hopes of refreshing his sense of self,
though no matter where he ventured from this
point,
no matter how involved he may be with another
woman,
there was still one ever so present,
in the flesh among the breathers,
with his last name hyphened after hers,
and she wasn't willing to let him go,
at least not on his own accord.

Wednesday Night's Dinner Special

As I blend the sorbet of shame
in the kitchen of doubt,
I wonder why you haven't finished
your pork and lie pie.

Maybe you're full from the plate of sorries
and last minute excuses.
Maybe it was the side order of
I Didn't Want You To Find Out Like This
topped off with whipped
It Didn't Mean Anything.

It never means anything.
Until I'm forced to swallow
a glass of cold truth
to dilute the hot
bowl of denial
I ravaged before.

I baked you trust,
and you ate it.
With more crumbs
on your lap than your mouth.

I grilled you portions
of passion meant to fill you,
to stave off
your insatiable appetite.

I guess I should've made
Whore rolls
with a pinch
of skank cinnamon

to curb your sweet tooth.

Now the oven is singed
with the ashes
of what our love was.

Your Stupidity Is Embarrassing Both of Us

I wonder about your mind,
that minute mass between your ears,
that thing reserved for intelligible thoughts.
Is it working?
Because from over here,
it appears to be out of order,
or maybe it was never activated to begin with.
I ask,
you see,
out of concern,
for your emotional and mental health.
You asking me to wrong something legally
right,
is not only an insult to my intelligence,
but a blow to yours as well.
I will not pet a rabid dog,
or cry for the devil,
so why do you expect me to start now?

She Eats from His Plate, and Samples Others

I was a mistake,
so she says,
though her sandstone eyes
say different.
I can only be a friend,
she exclaims,
though her lips tremble
with lust.
I was something to do,
she lies,
as her hands ache
to caress the bust
she's feasted upon,
and her belly stumbles
at the heated thoughts,
of our once
intermingled flesh.
I don't want to let her go,
but Jesus tells her so,
that what I am is wrong,
what we had is gone,
and to save
her soul,
she must cast me out,
like coal.

Bed Sheets

Doxy of the Opaque

She is one of pure confidence
Hands full of elegance
Wrists bathed in trinkets
Ears stained of stones

He is savoring her from afar
Parked in a friends car
Intrigued by what she is
Knowing his true intent

Leaning against an old building she is
Mouth dripping with sophistication
Dress woven of sin and lure
Eyes of twenty-four carat gold

Pupils meet and divide
He gazes but not miles
She sustains her mark

He peeks at this centerfold
Patent heels of infinity close in
Tingling engrosses his torso
While her figure soaks his sight

A wink and beam of milk
A pomegranate face
He lets the window descend
Words of candy are swallowed

The passenger door exhales
Her body inhales
The sedan tiptoes into the opaque

Where base Eves fly
And ravenous Adams die

False Advertisement

It's one thing to wear make up
but another to wear padded bras,
colored contacts, and rear enhancers.

If you wash or sweat your make up off,
it's no big deal.
But when it's time to satisfy
your carnal urges,
the question of where your
tits and ass went, will
be more perplexing,
than an Irish Setter
at a Tabby retreat.

Hot Silhouette

Across from me I stare,
at the shadow that's bare,
tossing its mane and torso,
If I could reach,
I'd never let go.
But I must close my blinds,
and redress my mind.

My Favorite Position

Beetle bumping?

Lizard lunging?

Snail Smacking?

Kitty crackn'?

I guess doggy style just sounds better.

The Prettiest Hooker I Know

1   She never wears pearls; they age her prim
appearance. Rubies, sapphires, emeralds, and
diamonds are all fair game. Whenever I see
her, I am hypnotized by the jewels, the
hardened facets of rainbows, that dress her
neck, wrists, ears, and fingers, like shards
of stained glass.

2   False eyelashes, yes. Mascara, no, unless
her clutch is dry, or the corner store is out
of stock. Her eyelashes are drapes to the
windows of her anima, those eyes flicker and
fade, like a dying star at midnight, in
Cameroon.

3   I don't know her last name, she never told
me. All I know is that her first name is
Heather, a name she says with an acid tongue.
She feels it's too "Anglo" for her, so she
told me once. Her street name is Bella, since
she loves Italian food, particularly the wine.
The taste drowns out her distaste for the sour
moments in life.

4   Bella only wears black wigs; she feels
blonde is overdone, red isn't that hot, and
brown is the same color as shit. She refuses
to walk around with a styled dog pile on her
head.

5   The wind whips up her nylon blend dress,
revealing beaten black-laced panties that
barely cover her lush, latte bum. She doesn't

refute the breezy intervention; it is a cool
intrusion of sweet relief from the humid,
uncouth, summer air. A blue late-model pickup
truck hesitates, as the driver fills his eyes
with Bella's moment of unsolicited favor.

6 There are so many pimps, the managers of
anatomical sales. Some are flashy, draped
with skins and furs of helpless victims;
jewelry heavier than their hands on the face
of a whore, and coifs so well cared for, the
rain thinks twice before brushing it. Others
are abrasive with words of never ending
onslaught at their girls, feeling the volley
of good business practices slink between the
voids of their fingers. To these pimps, a
pitcher's hand is more expensive to a whore,
than a show of uncommon metals and guises,
worth more than his shabby sense of values.
Bella is her own pimp, one that is a decent
medium, a lively merger of the aforementioned
types.

7 Her history is not a civil one; it's shaded
with bruises, bandages, and vast testaments of
why the only thing a human can love, is
paperweight. Heather is the daughter of
Peyton, a broccoli-eyed shell of a woman, and
Eli, a bark-skinned wandering soul, shackled
by the chains of Jim Crow, pressed by the
anvils of inequality. Nine years after
Heather's appearance, Peyton carved Eli after
she carved a chicken. The initial hysteria
upon little Heather, who had witnessed the
gory panorama, impelled Peyton to try and
carve the girl too. Instead, after wearing

herself with chase, she figured it best to carve herself.

8 To she who witnessed a once burning passion molt into ashes of heterogamy, she didn't sense the cents wanted to pay for love. It was always better to give than receive, though you stand to lose more, when you offer any portion of your beating, clotted, mass of veins and tissue. To give, is to declare a war of sharing.

9 Another John, another pence, another reflux of abandonment.

10 Being pretty is its own paroxysm.

Virgin Cocktail

MEET ME BEHIND THE OLD OAK TREE @ 10
read the lightly crumpled note
that traveled four desks over.
She knows why.
She knows what he wants.

The flash of butter bra
and lemon panties in Home Ec.
Now he wants some lemonade
and butter cookies.
Fourteen years
of honey
stored in a jar,
would be eaten
by a poppy-seeded
boy tagged Devereaux
who could barely speak
proper English,
let alone French.

He touched many breasts before,
mangos, kiwis, apples, melons, even grapes.
Yes grapes.
But only once did he get wine
from those.
Beer was much better.
Prue, the malt
of his dreams,
was cold and uncapped,
waiting to be stroked
and guzzled.

Devereaux had never licked
a beer tab
let alone sipped such drink,
but he knew Prue
could and would
slake his
barley thirst.

Drops rained on his boxers
as he pictured her,
lying there under that
beaten old oak,
who's had more
than it's share
of tasting parties
by its roots.
The butter melting,
lemon squeezing,
caused his tap
to lift,
inch by inch
until it held steady.

She was still there,
wondering why
the moon
looked like a cookie,
asking why
the sky
was bigger
than her ring collection.
What was it like
to unstop a keg
or uncork wine?

All she ever drank
Was pop
And milk.

Movement.
Groaning grass.
Devereaux appears.
Prue brightens.
He grins
from fear
and fervor.
She speaks
since she has no idea
what else to do.

He is thirsty.
She dehydrated.

Tears

Sparkless

It's hard watching someone
drown in their tears,
bound by the torture
grating their tender heart.
Offer words of amour and life,
trust it's enough to subside
the oozing of each wound.
Even if it's only for a pinch of time.
It is with love,
that your agony is my agony,
to carry on a back carved
with piquant memories,
and kiln-burned regrets.

Seasons of Amity

It is spring;
I hear the jittery pollen,
The sun's cheer,
The sky's chuckle,
squirrel perversions.
Our friendship is a babe,
Swaddled with coos and beams,
Feeding off breast nectar.
This babe's skin is hemp,
Hair of cashmere.

It is summer;
I smell the new berries,
The shy rivers,
The social fly,
squirrel chatter.
This friendship is a youth,
It gossips with me,
Even about me when I'm gone.
This youth's skin is nylon,
Hair of cotton.

It is autumn;
I see the orphaned leaves,
The cool wafts,
restless beetles,
the squirrel whispers.
Our friendship is an adult,
Pushing and loathing,
Stubborn but faint.
This adult's skin is burlap,
Hair is denim.

It is winter.
I feel the stillness of air,
The timed silence,
The derelict warmth,
the squirrel unseen.
This friendship has passed,
with the dust it goes,
the faux joys,
the firewood,
the faded hearts.
The skin is weathered,
The hair, no more.

Intersextion

Seated at a wooden banquet table,
is an intersexed human,
with their heart out,
to slice in even parts.
A part for mother who cries daily,
a part for father who denies nightly,
a part for sister who belittles boldly,
a part for brother who shames quietly.
There is still half of the heart left,
saved for all the friends who
look away when passing,
who mock in the evening,
and swoon at noon.
There it is, in all of its
blue-veined glory,
on a platter of stem cells,
properly portioned,
with no one
to carry out.

Descension to Hades

I've descended to the topsoil of demonic
planes,
where the price of one's fruits is the price
of another's pains.

The untamed forces of sadistic praise,
flay innocents of tragedy for hourless days.

Though the smoke of corpses and morality hang
freely,
my soul feels bounded by wired ropes and
thread that is steely.

The coat of cooking flesh over my bones begins
to melt,
the fires around me heighten, growl, and welt.

Enforcing more heat onto my broiled frame,
all my limbs and tired neck go lame.

For now it is done.
The sadist has won.

A spirit of beaten and scratched amnesty,
is now a mere defunct fantasy.

Black Bombazine

Woe is she,
with bombazine.
In the night,
of inky clean.
It matches her,
with shades of black.
From the tip of her bonnet,
to the curls down her back.
She aches like a heathen,
a true stoned pagan.
As she curses God,
and questions Satan.
For her heart has been,
arcane with burns.
The dry words leave her mouth,
as the old voices carry.
Her love is gone,
way down below.
Where flames are high,
and morals are low.

Heavy Things

Such heavy things,
we mortals lift,
to keep the weight
of the inevitable,
off our backs.

Cue Cards

What Shall I Do With My Eyes?

They've seen so much, maybe too much.
The agony of unbridled violence amongst a
population fighting a cold war,
another mother blinded by the umbilical cord
of her first born,
who now ravages her savings account, for a fix
with diffused perceptions.
Same country bleeding out all the corruption,
bit by bit,
with each head of every citizen on a stick!
Poor little offspring,
begging unknown deities for scratch and
pillows.

Slander!
Slander!
Slander!

The president, the queen, the prime minister
and chiefs are all in bed together,
playing naked Twister between sips of urine
tainted Merlot,
and bites of aging pumpernickel.

So what shall I do with my eyes?
It may be best to pluck them out,
out of this very head whose ears collect
mantra,
diatribe,
sarcasm,
songs,
pleas,
speeches,

and
lactose lies.

More!
More!
More!

The Bright Side

1. When life gives you limes, make mojitos.
2. When life gives you money, spend a little and save a lot.
3. When life gives you rabbits, don't make stew. A hat and gloves will do you better.
4. When life gives you whores, strap up or pull out.

Yes, You're A Pagan

Christmas is now Xmas. I blame society.

About Spiders

If it's black,
then attack!

If it's brown,
take it down!

If it's tan,
let it stand!

The Report Card

Realizing P.E. really stands for ~~Punishing Everyone~~ Physical Exigency |B+|

Knowing that algebra, geometry, calculus, and other intricate arithmetic is useless to the average person |A-|

Science is only fun when you don't have to read or write anything |C+|

Even English teachers don't speak English well |A+|

Art classes should have only two grades: P or F (Pass or Fail) |B+|

All music is meant for head banging or break dancing |B-|

Labels

white   homophobic   slut
gay   black   virgin
red   old   pervert
lazy   brown   drunk
prude   ugly   nerd
fat   stupid   bitch
psycho   ginger   atheist
snobby   brunette   racist
yellow   phony   sexist
ghetto   blonde   stoner
poor   city   girl
rich   country   boy
free   american   vegan
submissive   greedy   child
french   unemployed   smoker
asian   small   non-smoker
big   african   athlete
latino   democrat   student
strong   illiterate   immigrant
loud   conservative   muslim
quiet   republican   christian
educated   liberal   convict

Products should have labels, not people.

Spots

I, Myself, and Me

I know what's been done and what people told
Me, but is there steady strength within
Myself when someone challenges who
I am? Is it enough for
Me to have confidence beyond consciousness?
To relieve
Myself if the time calls for it?
I may only be
Me when all that's left is
Myself.

Human Sacrilege

To think, when we were only mere molecules, we were
good, clean, happy, and sheltered with
rhinestone blankets.
Then, in the corners of humanity, we're slowly
injected with
bowls of treason and bits of ignorance.

They say one sex can't be equal to another.
They say one race can't be equal to another.
They say one dollar can't be equal to another
dollar.
They say one love can't be equal to another
love.
They say one formula can't be equal to
another.
They say one human can't be equal to another.

These pints of loathing and quarts of
malevolence,
all but escape our souls as they go under,
beyond the Earth's layers,
to simmer at the liquid core,
where the bland steam and sour smoke,
will rise to filter once again.

From Toy Phones to iPhones

It's over.
The endless cartoon binges
The rides on the big wheel
The grass stained jeans
The mom-cooked meal.
The Barbie Fun House
The Ninja Turtle dudes
The grandma jewelry
The dad-grilled foods.
The stale Halloween candy
The stones at the creek
The glazed donut holes
The thrills of hide and seek.
The regular Nintendo
The shark game in the pool
The fear of Chucky
The end of elementary school.

It begins.
The incoming messages
The coffee in the morning
The slips and suits
The last verbal warning.
The broken condoms
The first crazy ex
The pregnancy test
The lack of sex.
The child support
The unpaid bill
The lap dances
The shoot to thrill.
The office politics
The endless fights

The trending topics
The sleepless nights.

The Sins of Social Networking

The Internet has birthed social networking,
Something that is and isn't working.

With the likes of Twitter, Facebook, and
MySpace,
I can't avoid seeing everyone's digiface.
Tweeting about that damn Lohan.
Posting about the fray of Kanye.
Like like like.
I'll accept your friend request,
but ignore his.
Retweet that,
and favorite this.
Uh oh! Another trashy bathroom pic.
I just got deleted off someone's friend list.
Be a pop star on YouTube,
or a porn star on RedTube.
Tag people on Facebook,
and lol on Lamebook.
Did someone just say they're at the abortion
clinic?
You just admitted that guy hit and quit it.
Why would you post all that shit on your wall?
Now everyone is lls at both of y'all.
Some things really should stay private,
TMI is well provided.
Back away from the keyboard,
hands off the smartphone.

Have fun on the Internet,
don't be daft on the internet,
unless you're a punk.

To Be Quixotic

Believing in never ending romance,
though divorce is the new marriage.
Feeling school is a waste of time,
since I don't apply myself,
and thereby deny myself,
a chance at a light of lime.
Seeing a rich man on the most scathing corner,
of the most hardened street,
in the most dilapidated city,
with a hat turned over,
in his overturned hand,
panhandling like an expert hobo.
Watching a young girl dance half covered for
cash,
because it beats doing anything else.

Eve's Regret

I almost died yesterday,
Right there in the lab
When my apple pie
Became cherry.
I'll never wear white bottoms again;
Not as long as I'm a woman.

White bottoms are for girls
Since girls don't get
Cramps
Nausea
Fatigue
Diarrhea
Or
Upset stomachs
Or Abnormal appetites
For processed
Cocoa products.

If I'm a woman now,
Than why must I
wear a diaper?
It isn't large
Or cumbersome,
But it still has to be changed
And reeks of bloody torment.

I nearly cried yesterday,
In a closed bathroom stall
As I tied my hoodie around my waist;
A temporary bandage
For my wound of
Womanhood,

A newfound journey
Of Midol laced naps
Sucrose binges
And PMS rants.

The Middle-Aged Man Enrolled in Western Philosophy

Sometimes it's never enough.
You study in the morning, at lunch, and before
bed.
You read more than the minimum chapters.
You write a few extra pages on your term
paper,
in hopes that your professor won't deem you,
a lazy shmuck with thinning hair and a thick
neck,
all for the struggle of succession.

I Need More Than Soap to Be Clean

I need more than soap to be clean,
if I want an aura of calla lily.
My soul must be polished
with untainted affection
and saccharine intentions.
My heart must be hollow,
so that love and serene promises
may fill it.
My mind must be clear as autumn skies,
with no remnants of styptic scores
and bludgeoned bridges.
I need more than soap to be clean,
for peace is scarce,
and sin is abundant.

Truth

I like your shoes
better than you,
which is
saying a lot,
since the
shoes don't
flatter
your feet.

Someone's in the House

I heard something, then realized it was just a
huge housefly, trapped between the blinds and
the window of the bathroom.

What a ruckus in a house with only one
occupant.

The Resting Age

The body cascades down a valley of restless
hills,
trying to catch hold of momenta tranquility.
The supple armor is tended to in royal
fashion,
with hands of apricot flesh,
as liquids of various essences,
sate each pore.
The eyelids bounce lightly as the hips
protrude,
signaling the commencement of unconscious
cinema.
A light gown wraps the frame.
adding more pleasure to the eyes of the moon.
Now the body lies still,
as the mind wades in ponds of freesia.

Sun In My Eye

Rays
so
luminous,
like
ametrine,
glamorous.

About the Author

Justine Monikue possesses a BFA in digital design, and an MFA in creative writing. Her first poem, *I Am Nature*, was published in the *Anthology of Poetry by Young Americans: 1995 Edition*, when she was ten years old. Her short story, *Up In Smoke*, has been published in *Morning Stories*, a collection of various fictional works. She currently resides in Delaware with her two children. You can connect more with Justine on her blog at jfilez.wordpress.com.